MAROON

poems by
Danielle Legros Georges

CURBSTONE PRESS

Printed on acid-free paper by Transcontinental Book Group/ Best
Book Manufacturing
Cover design: Stone Graphics

This book was published with the support of the
Connecticut Commission on the Arts and donations
from many individuals. We are very grateful for this
support.

Library of Congress Cataloging-in-Publication Data:

Georges, Danielle Legros.
    Maroon / by Danielle Legros Georges.— 1st ed.
      p. cm.
    ISBN 1-880684-79-9 (pbk.)
    1. Haitian Americans—Poetry. 2. Haiti—Poetry.   I. Title.
  PS3607.E67 M37 2001
    811'.6—dc21   2001028529
  Printed in Canada
  Published by
  CURBSTONE PRESS
  321 Jackson St.
  Willimantic, CT 06226 • info@curbstone.org • www.curbstone.org

Acknowledgments

Grateful acknowledgment is made to the editors of the following publications in which these poems first appeared, some in slightly different form:

Abafazi: "Looking Up"
Agni: "A Cut"
Artist and Influence: "A Painting at the Met" and "General Sun"
Black Renaissance/Renaissance Noire: "Hen Hen Hen," "Maroon," and "Stones for Libations"
Calabash: "Anacaona" and "Fillette"
The Caribbean Writer: "Another Ode to Salt" and "small i"
The Christian Science Monitor: "Airfield"
Compost: "To and From"
The Journal of Modern Writing: "Accents in Degrees"
MaComère: "Fishing," "How to Kiss," "musing" (originally appeared in a scholarly article by Kathleen Balutansky), "Night Watch," and "Praisesong for Port-au-Prince"
Obsidian: "Fin Wè Mò," "Grasshopper," "My Father is Dogon," and "Ogoun"
pen·umbra: a collection of poetry by women of color: "Vellum"
Step Into a World: A Global Anthology of the New Black Literature: "The Yellow Forms of Paradise"
Tanbou/Tambour: "Mrs. Jean Louis Listens to the Doctor, Boston City Hospital" and "The List Grows"
Yemassee: "Our Water"

For my mother and grandmother,
and in the memory of my father.

Please note: Some of the poems contain words or phrases in Haitian Creole, French, or Spanish. Their English translations appear in a glossary at the end of the book, along with notes.

Contents

I.   To and From / 3

Buttercup / 5

A Dream: The Clock Is Melting / 6

Songs For Women / 7

Hen Hen Hen / 8

musing / 10

palimpsest dress / 11

Night Watch / 12

Attached / 14

Maroon / 15

Fishing / 17

small i / 20

How to Kiss / 22

A Painting at the Met / 24

II.   Another Ode to Salt / 27

Boston Back Yard / 28

Mrs. Jean-Louis Listens to the Doctor,
               Boston City Hospital / 29

Family Portrait / 30

Airfield / 31

Accents in Degrees / 32

Stones for Libations / 33

My Father is Dogon / 35

Anacaona / 36

Nova / 39

The List Grows / 40

Vellum / 41

Praisesong for Port-au-Prince / 42

Fin Wè Mò / 43

St. Francesco / 46

Ogoun / 47

General Sun / 48

III.   Vexed / 51

Compas / 54

Fillette / 55

Looking Up / 56

Our Water / 57

Writing Lesson on the Lawn / 58

IV.   Everyone Loves a Good Villain / 61

A Cut / 62

At the Basketball Hall of Fame / 63

Grasshopper / 65

Hostage / 67

The Yellow Forms of Paradise / 68

Notes / 71

Maroon

I

To and From

She laughs and recounts their escape
from the rural region where they'd built their farm
of chickens and goats, rice fields, some beans.

Despite not being a market woman, she'd been shrewd,
forced to be, in a country ruled by anticipation

of food shortages,
of shortages of gasoline,
of shortages
of electricity,
shortages of power,
of power shifts.

Her husband, in his impeccable restraint, recounts
their consideration of the hen-house as refuge,
behind the barbed wire or in the plantain fields
where humans and trees are often confused at night,

while the gunmen, if they came this time,
shot the house, perhaps the dog in the yard,
indiscriminate as the circulating lists of the marked:

radio announcers,
teachers,
students and
the religious,
so-and-so Jean Baptiste,
followed by
woman of so-and-so
Jean Baptiste.

The woman and man laugh a nervous laugh
at their daring: how at rooster's crow they crept
into their station wagon and through the hills
of Plaisance, down the coast into Gonaives
where their old church stood (sign-of-the-cross),
through the Raboteau the army dared not enter,

where the people threw back the clothes the governors
had brought, threw foreign rice into canals. They drove
quickly around the salted hills, like country-bus drivers,
like all the country's drivers, this time not speeding
for market or goats or grain but for the capital
where anonymity would protect them.

Buttercup

How to imagine
Those places where chaos holds sway
—Linda Hull

would begin in a buttercup field,
face-down in buttercups,
the earth in your nostrils,
a dampening of sky on your back,
rain
                in palomino sheets,
and cows so far that nature turns
into this plot, this green, and you
take it in silent swallows,
in the dandelion milk
fixing your fingers, and burrs
fastened to your pant legs.

Where chaos holds sway
is not dark but light, light
gasps, the surface breathing
of a cantaloupe, and inside
orange liver, orange lungs,
orange heart

of a cantaloupe
picnic-tabled on a paper plate
under a tent of mashed potatoes
with gravy sidling down
— but no real hunger for these
when you've reached the clearing,
after the field, past the "where
on earth have you been"s
and the how to say where
or say how the earth pulled you
in and spit you out stunned.

A Dream: The Clock is Melting

The clock's green digits spill into the room's berylline
midnight in the dream. They leave a trail, phosphorescence,
the way sulphur leaves a corpse.

Time is liquid then, melts, undemarcates itself from important events,
say, the turn of the school-year with leaves, the day one's image
(say "cheese") is taken for the local paper.

I take the dream to mean that age blurs distinctions and as time
goes, life turns into itself, and the end of a life is its beginning,
and the flash of a life's breadth: a single breath, expelled light,
for the fifteenth time,

or the first, which may be like eyeing a star, which is, of course,
dead, thousands of light years away and ago. And it is so
that a passed parent becomes an ancestor and so that that ancestor

melts into a god, and so that the past can embody a now
as real as the room's blue backdrop for the melting
green numbers.

Songs for Women

I will there be no women here
who would circle red-
dressed, ruby-hearted,

glass-cut. If there be flowers,
then the bloom of cyclamen
awned in green's glowing
night-vase, night-shade,

wild in wind. Sin be the will
to descend, humming-bird still,
steal the fire's sound, take note

and return it. Let song be
the skin of a glimmering,
unsettled, razing, belly-deep
in the strike of match and band.

Be the belly, the pepper-pot.
Come close just to drop it.
Slide 'til the notes are a scaffold,
ash-flicked, unphoenixed.

Hen Hen Hen

A dive from tree
from rock and rock

skipping like an aged heart
chained to machinery

a running hum the strum
of a life chord plucked.

Still feet warm heart
cold feet heart jumps rope

hope skips a rocket's purr
pierces twilight.

Flight the wind supreme
rooftops dreideling

blue-green marble worlds
swallowed like pills.

Pills? Pillbox church-hats
and steeple spires

are dots from here.
Keep the beam

not to drop
to bob untethered

unrepentant.
Look! Icarus rising.

No, woman metal-winged.
Flighty hincty maybe

but flapping yes shaking
off the chick-bird tree.

Cat-calls fall flat
to her ear to wind

she hatched for speed
for cruise above rooster's

crow. *Kookoorookooroo*
don't wantchu anyway

they say and puff
it up peck at plumes

fume.
Well.

Hen hen hen
sistren

wing and work
a thing

bring and gather
band waists

croon:

make haste
make haste

flying lessons
starting now.

musing

the muse licks her own tongue
pens rhymes for her own pleasure
dips her quill,
                              mind-stick
                              in dark ink
                              of her skin
and sits at a large bureau thinking

palimpsest dress

rests on
a hanger — silver
shape
meaning
to be
shoulders —
whose
neck
stems, bends
about a bar
that holds
the armoire up

palimpsest dress
bias-cut
diasporic
(travels well)
hand-sewn
hems, darts,
(suitably)
to the stole's
left, the bustier's
right

palimpsest dress
which type of woman
slips you on
ink-spot
and all?

Night Watch

The old woman has turned her ire on me.
I am a symbol to her, an evil,
the daughter she never had
or never wanted
to have.
Dead,
I'd be
more useful
to her. The nails
and hammer she seeks tonight
would build a coffin, a boat
in which to float me away.

         Was it so long ago
         that she'd spread a blanket in sand,
         the shoots of the day turning the world
         to spring, and her husband there, and her
         own mother there, and despite the elder's glare,
         the water and air playing into light,
         into frenzy, and in her heart all was alive.

Stills, they are stills, the woman
says. I see my life before me
as if in a movie.
The film rolls
quickly.
I don't believe myself
this age, and yet I am this age.

         This night she paints her nails a deep violet
         and calls back the indigo placed in slats,
         the tap, tap, tap, and scrape of the violet-grey matter

into wooden squares, the dye into
the white fabric ready for color.

Unraveling is a basket of blue clothes
to be ironed, a mountain of blue
and a hand curled around
the iron,
around its leaden weight,
her fingers curled around a cloth
around the handle beside a mountain

          of blue skirts, blue jeans, the blue
          of a seemingly never-ending day,
          blue and everlasting day, the blue
          of an almost-blue hibiscus, blue of irises,
          her now-iris-rimmed eyes, and the flowers
          themselves on her dresser.

She is swift to name what destroys her:
My mind is clear, yet my body
crumbles. My memory
crumbles, yet
my mind
is clear.
I can move so
quickly through time.

          The irises I've placed on her dresser and know
          I have little time to find how her time tied
          her body to pain, how she tied the pain
          to her body, how she knew her mind surpassed her
          time and became a curse and how girls became curses
          and crosses to bear. I bear my cross with her.
          I take on her anger — one thread to her story.

Attached

for William Decillien
and the spider-cart haulers
of Port-au-Prince

Attached to the cart
are two sacks.

Attached to the sacks
is a mountain

I am hauling. Attached
to my back

is the cart. My bare soles
are as coarse

as the road. I could be
a horse:

stepping yet trapped.

Maroon

Bareback on the river of blood...
—Aimé Césaire

Some say where mountains

take root   red blooms

pierces through rock   makes

a haven   a way of life

a way to say   "maroon"

the colored handle of a single-edged saber

or   "crimson"

the sword itself

blue in its red distinction.

To touch these words to lip or belly

to arm

is to ask of a mountain its dead

who rise not whole but bit by bit:

an ear severed from sound

two hands left to a wooden stump

a body bloated in the water of its motion.

Mention "lap of wave"

and the sea becomes a monument

of bones walking backward

and we, the skin of the waves.

Utter "palm-tree" or "mango"

(in ease) and beyond each springs

a witness killed for her eyes,

and the ripe fruit, new eyes

that wave in the breeze.

This way of saying	of seeing
this rounding	of mountain
the boring	through it
for font	for fountain-pen
for arm	
	takes root
pierces through rock	makes
a way	of life
a way to say	maroon.

Fishing

psychoalphadiscobetabioaquadooloop
    —George Clinton, *Aquaboogie*

The first word learned
in this language: *fish.*

My eyes: sharks poised
at mouth openings

to feed when lips and teeth
engaged tongue to propel

sound forward. I gulped
greedy for decoding,

my new world
tongue coated

curled about
inflexible consonants

like a great whale exerting
its continental tail.

Here lights that
"turn off"

and don't
"close"

turn
notions

17

of wicks
in oil

to neon
strobes

and light
waves

away the world
almost I know.

The swing of this
new speech comes

hard like a swim stroke
through ice

like an arm akimbo
on a salty girl's hip

at a disco.
A minnow I

surefooted dance
arm about

the predator's neck.
He in a sharkskin suit

moves forward
a slippery foot

dissolves
in light then turns

returns dissolves
to stir a tango

of idiom. Each flip
of his foot grounds

each flip of my foot
seeking ground, I say:

fout! He says:
Now the dance.

small i

this symbol (i):
a cymbal
streak to sun
pole and stop-sign
stick and circle-never-ceasing

its dot: eternal eye
never ceasing to see
two *c*'s
touching lips

an open mouth in prayer
an *o* not *majuscule*

the small *i* unegoed

* * *

As children we went
from print to script
on yellow paper ruled
like the roads crossed
to school.

A line was two
parallel paths
for ascenders,
descenders.

* * *

School nights beneath a lamp-post,
my mother, a girl, is learning
to count, not stars, but
figures with the others in the dark,

un et un
                    — deux
deux et deux
                    — quatre

in quatrain of songs set to learn
facts aren't earth, aren't dirt
to be digging, are a desk,
are a trade to be traded
for fields.

Her mother figured she would measure
infinitely, and counted on her counting
to keep her free.

Me, she led to the word as puzzle,
as game to ungag the number of times
she'd stood unworded. She decided
to start in the midst of things,
leaving *a* and *e*, picking up
small *i*.

How to Kiss

The children know how to kiss,
to descend stairwells when called
into rooms of coloured lips

whispered *entendres,* demure smiles,
the uncle who *an Kreyol* calls us
"kochon mawon," "wild pigs."

We walk into crooned *comment vas tu*
*uu*s rolling too long from gold-filled mouths,
thistly jowls. We kiss

the cheek, the next cheek, and more
cheeks, the odors of Vitalis
(the smart man's hair tonic),

of Bain de Champagne, Chanel No. 5,
Eau de Floride, of various adult *eaus.*
We bristle in advance against the teenager

whose five-o'-clock shadow goes from sun-yard
to sit in parlors, his knees eclipsed in cloth,
a foreshadow that we too would be the kissed.

But Pascale had the audacity, once,
to alter form, opening her mouth
to snake a tongue that swept

beige powder from the face of Madame
Altagrâce LaVache, exposing a patch
of brown from chin to ear.

"Un véritable scandale."

"Tongue on cheek?!"

"Truth indeed, the wild pigs!"

A Painting at the Met

They are all four astride a horse.
The woman almost looking back
over the small child she clasps.

The man, in front, holds a boy
in one arm, the reins in the other.

They are fleeing something vast,
the map on which their bodies figure.
It is the 19th century. They are black.

I see: The ashen color of their clothes,
the dread that composes the woman's face,
the grip of distress in the man's holding
the horse steady. They are bold. I don't
know that, for them, there exists a choice.

Flight writes itself on their backs.

II

Another Ode to Salt

We navigate snow not ours
but grown used to, one cold foot
over another, adopt accoutrements:
a red scarf, wind-wrapped and tight,
boots, their soles teethed like sharks,
shackling our ebon ankles, the weight
of wool coats borrowed from
nos ancêtres, les Gaulois.

Masters at this now,
we circumvent ice
as we do time, reach home.

The salt you bend to cast
parts the snow around us.
I bend, and think
of a primary sea,
harbors of danger and history,
passing through the middle
in boats a-sail in furious storms,
cargo heavy,
of *mystères,* renamed,
submerged and sure,
riding dark waves,
floating long waves
to the other side of the water
and the other side
and the next.

Boston Back Yard

The image of the headless hen
depends on the wring.
My grandmother puts her hands
on the thing, is ginger.
A simple dust rises from the yard.

We'd been playing too long inside
and escaped to the porch.
She'd not meant us to see the white feathers
pinking, the twisting this way
and that of the run, the tree
as it threatened the racer.

My grandmother wipes her hands
on her apron, which is blue
with white buttons, and touches the dust
to pick up the hen.
She speaks but two words, which are soft,
to the bird, to the wind,
she sends one word of thanks.

Mrs. Jean-Louis Listens to the Doctor, Boston City Hospital

The red mark on your daughter's cheek
is not a birthmark, but a parasite,
says the doctor.

He reiterates, "A PAR-A-SITE."

"Most people in the world
live with parasites," he adds.
"Here, we are lucky."

Family Portrait

It's funny, in the photo,
that my father is missing.

He is the photographer;
he will always be missing

in action with the American
friends who will be his

distractions; later in the arms
of cancer; and later still

away and ago. We gaze
into his eyes through the lens

of mother, wife, daughter,
while my three brothers

are busy building something
in the ground of this first

snow. We are *Haitiens*
dressed for our first snow

still *Haitiens* then,
in our first snow.

Airfield

I recall looking out onto an airfield
with my father (at age five),
his shoulders lifting me to the night sky,
his head, a world I sat above
to better see the field below us.

Planes became stars, first
red-dwarfed lights, then roar.
My delight (of course) was that their might
came so close to matching his.

Accents in Degrees

On the green porch, a woman
disperses the silence of night
with a paper fan.

A girl, in spite of mosquitoes,
watches the moon's white
half crescent rise.

In the doorway, a man
silhouettes himself
and smokes.

His cigarette drifts inside
past a boy asleep
beneath a yellow net.

Between the four, accents
in degrees to which they will
become attached to each other

and this damp night
in Kinshasa, 1970, far from
the Jacmel they left

and the Montreal now
where the girl who watched
the moon writes her mother

with news of her brother
abroad and shuts out
the moon's light.

Stones for Libations

It's after many years
I come here,
hoping;

not sure what
I hope for, a stone
in one hand,

the other rubbing
itself as if easing
prayer.

Sorrow
wipes
my forehead.

My mother and I
choose this day,
winds whipping,

heat up, trees
singing, to visit
this place

inscribed
with the names
of those

who will remain.

We will not,
but these stones
in our palms

remind us
that here
one can be

anything,
that tradition
is dictated

by place,
and when
in Rome . . .

So I place
my small stone
on your tombstone

Father,

asking these gods
and ours
for balm.

My Father is Dogon

My father is Dogon.
I know this to be true.
I see him in the face
of a man I see walking
on Flatbush Avenue.

To him I say only,
"You look like my father,"
to which he says only,
"I am Dogon."

My father is Dogon.
I know this to be true.
I see him in the face
of a man I see walking
on Flatbush Avenue.

I have no other proof.

Anacaona

... and my name will be dropped
                        golden leaf
                        flower

voice of gold

                        the gold

of mountains beyond mountains
I've crossed to behold my own

                        face

despite my body's death
in double cross
(by a Spanish gentleman's deal:
the sword/the crucifix)

despite divisions of time
of tribes   Taino
                        Carib...

the island's body itself
its zones:

        Marien
                        Magua

        Maguana   Higuey

Xaragua

engulfed
transfigured
my own children

         scattered

the *sanba*

           lost

their tongues

       scattered

my name buried by music
foreign to me

the mountain-sides bursting
in red

my gestures   marooned

    I have seen what will be
the mirroring gaze through time
      the sun in eclipse
      reflection and

        reflection
an imprint
       of my face
the study of
      my aim

and my name will sow maize
my name will breed vision
my girls will be black, bronzed,
their eyes will be storms

and my name dropped
golden leaf
flower

voice of gold
the gold
of mountains
beyond mountains
I've crossed
to behold my own face.

Nova

based on a vodou lamentation

they say it is death
to look upon the star
the star brings death

the sickness called your name
I saw it pass us by
now look at us here
a sign for the living

the brightness flashed over us
it curved around our names
it arched this hand of death
Death's arm curved around us
now look upon our misery

today we are changed
look upon the misery
that has changed us
our words become stones
the stones are words around us
our words are pressed
as our hearts are pressed

they say it is death
curving its tongue
it is death they say
they say it is death

The List Grows

They sent you back by boat
to a familiar shore,

your son and daughter with you,
your wife had passed safely.

You hid first in Mirebalais,
then in Port-au-Prince

where they arrested you,
disappeared you for two days.

Yvon Desanges, I know only
of your voyage,

and your image after:
your brow missing each eye

your mouth without its tongue
your left ear lost to a field,

your face mined. Your face
remains beautiful.

It blazes to lay bare
your faceless assassins

who could not
disfigure you.

Vellum

All torturers should write books
on how fingers can be curled into vises,

on the exact location of joints
in relation to well-oiled machines,

on how to use pressure
to loosen tongues.

As writers formulate plots
using certain devices to best effect,

upon reflection, torturers should
direct their attention

to ensuring their details are correct
before writing the stories

of their victims — for perspective.

Praisesong for Port-au-Prince

Cold kills slowly.
One moves and keeps
moving until suddenly
an arm grows dead
then a foot falls off
and the torso freezes
as if submerged in chilled water,
ice and swimmer
forming a block.

It's a slow death,
never red or yellow
with guts hanging out
and decay that spreads
its blanket and birds
that descend with feathers
and beaks,
and finally peace:
efficient, spectacular.

You, city of the fast death,
of the bloody coup,
I bow to you.
For you I cut flowers
to put into a blue vase
of cold, clear water.

Fin Wè Mò

My Boston dead face

The deadness of my *âme*

The aim of my death

Death in the shape of a black butterfly

Upside down death

Death as it presents itself neatly

Pink background death

Egyptian pants of death

Breathless death

Irreverent death tapping its foot

Ringworm of death around the heart

Sanded death

A thousand thousand hours

Sun death comes to me in a sea anemone

Death of sand /of glass/of almond shells

This year's death

Who else? death

Bones of the goat

Foot of the sailor death

Death at the hand of a market woman's word

Death in the eyes of a tough child who will live

Super death wearing a long fur-trimmed coat

Les dents de la mer death

Night of stars

Death in a red night robe

Foxy death

Oooooo   oooooo to get off death

Pa Benyen Ni Ak Kilot Ni Ak Eslip death
on the *Plaj Piblik*

Pa Benyen Toutouni death

Death without teeth

Unleashed death

Death with the head of a dog

Pawed to death

Clean death with clean breath

The hot breath of death death

Leaving death's door

Monkey death

Made-up death

Abacus of death in the moment to moment

Momentous death/heroic death/Rubiconic death

Snake-eye death

Death of dice

Teething mice death

Goat death *beh beh*

St. Francesco

based on a detail, Basilica di S.Croce, Florence

Finches, finches everywhere,
by the fountain in the square.
Hooded monk, red book in hand,
spreads the word, by bird, to man.

Ogoun

A million birds sing
in the tower whose steeple

hoists a rooster into space.
The rooster — symbol of baptism,

of kings to others, of god
to some — struts, with fine crest

red, with violet underfeathers.
He lords his roost. We peck

at the meaning of truth
in the courtyard beneath

in academic speech.

But the blacksmith
who surely knew

sculpted this cocky beast
to be in all weathers vain,

as goad to god to strike
his metal wings with thunder.

No storm comes; the day
is fair, and Mr. Rooster

tips his beak
to the sweet, sweet air.

General Sun

The sun is a sly fellow
who sneaks into rooms
in darkness and pries
open eyes with a kiss.

He'll play tricks that form
fountains from sand
and should you find
these bland, he'll become

a burning orange bush,
take up the sky and blind
you before retiring
to ponder his incarnations.

III

Vexed

I'm vexed to love you . . .
The shape of returns
— Li-Young Lee

This place in which we love
holds no palm trees such as these
of a photograph

your father could have loved
my mother in and we the twins
of their shining

would be closer than we are
now that I am guarded
in your arms,

each of our nails cutting
a small death in the fist
of open and clenching.

My image of lovers drawn
before births and flights
from place

would have killed us,
yes — but you take
from the passings

of lives our love
like a thing plucked
from fire.

We were each born
in transport
that left our tongues

tied for years, that left
in your mouth a stutter
and in mine

a snakebite, a swollen
heart. *Pull it,*
I say, *pull it out,*

the abrupt stop
of trucks
in the night of a town

that sees
the child-you
on the floor

of your living room,
the windows cracked,
your father's face

breaking,
and I will give you
my mother's stare

in the face
of uncracking time,
her halting

silence.
We will grind
these to ashes

for a new cement.
We will crush them
to powder for glue.

I have sent
for the pestle,
the mortar, I leave to you.

Compas

Suddenly, with the chairs wheeled round,
the tables on their sides, the diners wedged
between edge of hall and stage, the band strikes
like a thief, pocketing all speech.

Elise rises, in a silver dress, Robert's hand
seizes his breast pocket, fumbles for something,
a pen, perhaps a handkerchief, to steady him
from his pulse.

My father is a fine dancer. His meringue feet
accumulate the drag and hesitation necessary
to dictate delirium when he leads my mother
in the dance:

He charms her into feeling she is young,
that they are themselves when they met
on the Champs de Mars, she in a similar dress,
but dove-colored and cut on the bias,

the color of his *mouchoir,*
he, with moustache trimmed dangerously.
She is sampling rum punch, is wearing white gloves,
is the sister of the most beautiful girl

in Gonaives, is a teacher at the Catholic school.
He, a young engineer with a flower
in his *boutonnière,* is flamboyant,
is disarming, has akimboed an arm around her,

has charmed her with his feet.

Fillette

According to my grandmother, when she was a *fillette,*
A third eye pierced her forehead from inside,
Like a knot of a fall from a rude bicycle.

She saw in a dream a roaring beast that would crawl
The earth in a blue trail of vapors, leaving behind it
A track of tears. On her nineteenth birthday

A ship discharged the town's first motorcar. She saw it
With her own eyes. It was bought by *Mr. You-Know-Who,*
The one they called *Direk.* Women, children, and men

In Panamas tipped so, stopped to watch the machine
With her and him in it spin down the rusting pier:
Iron red dashed by the end-of-day's marigold sun.

In the car they powdered the city's thin streets,
But it wasn't the headlights, my grandmother
Says, that cleared the path–It was her eye

Like a first Kenscoff star, that came out
and shone, while the town's candles,
left behind, wept in envy.

Looking Up

This afternoon sky,
its pink and orange clouds,
is cruel in its beauty,
and beneath it
you, so far from me.

What can I do
but insist that the sky change
color, that something dark
peek through this shimmering
cover.

Our Water

You said I have steps
in my hair when water falls
on it, curls flattening into squares
like rice paddies cut into mountains.

We could have been in a waterfall,
at the sacred site of Saute-D'eau,
encircled by an impromptu
ceremony of birds.

Instead, in Boston's November,
we take what we can:
flights of laughter,
and only a bar
of soap
between us.

Writing Lesson on the Lawn

It is yellow, the leaf
lying by your toe. A cigarette burns

in the grass. We write
what each of us knows to be true:

                              I write: You

lying there, the air drawing
moisture

to your hair-wishing-itself-a-mane.
The heat

stirring this game of watching,
writing,

deciding, aptly, on the leaf as point
of departure.

IV

Everyone Loves a Good Villain

the ones whose deeds elicit long and hushed
"no"s which deepen as the hole into which
our man or woman falls grows, because, face it:

We all want to know that we never could,
never can, would never, and at which point
does it matter which fiction we're fed,

we eat it up, what stands out there, our
other face. We jeer at the blackguard, go
out of our ways to poke the beast, and in

doing so release ourselves. Villains build
community. They tell us who we are.
They come outlined as a black boy

with a three-musketeers bar in his pocket.
He's thought to be packing a gun. Our
chocolate fantasy melts as he falls. We've

been trained. Shoot first, falter second.

We hate to lose our villains. We'd loved
them for hating them so. Letting go means
a piece of our skin peels from us. No more

baiting or thrill of the hunt, no more corners
into which we trap the villain, and when we
are done, the monster disarmed,

we do not know what to do with ourselves,
our hands lie beside themselves.

A Cut

based on "Katz Mit Vogel"
a painting by Pablo Picasso

In the cat's mouth
a dark wing
then a red tear

and the bird itself
suspended
beak unbroken.

Voices break
round a table
cut-up flutter.

But we go back
 to the cat's
claws.

The bird's mouth
releases. Silence again
seizes the thing.

Its squawk never reaches
its throat,
its stuttering wound

a breach of geometry
that leaves all impression
of flight.

At the Basketball Hall of Fame

The photo suspends him in mid-air:
legs unstressed, fingertips at opposite edges
of his sphere's circumference,

arms lazy but for gravity's claim
to their outstretched placement there,
each hand's under exposed, light.

In his face, all the tension
levitation has not allowed his body,
as if his eyes alone have willed the body "rise."

Cheeks engulfed with an enourmous breath,
and as he stares ahead
at the ball in its half-birth

through the hoop, this man
legs dark against his uniform
resembles Christ hung; the ball his god,

the basket's net collecting all expectation
and disbelief of this brilliant instant
of only him

                    and beyond him
the colossal arena,
the obscured spectators whose roars

force his lift, raise him, pin him up,
keep him in the second it takes
to capture him there

once, and for all time
until the photo fades, until the image
fades, until another dark figure appears

to take and hold the court breathless.

Grasshopper

I turn my head and say, "Ah, grasshopper."
I turn my head and say, "Ah, grasshopper,"
in imitation of the master who teaches
David Carradine that life is a series
of mountains to be destroyed
or resurrected in the imagination. Or
a blade of grass atop which titters
a water drop that sticks
to the hind legs
of an insect
that flits
across grass as if across water.

Water-crawler, with legs so light,
body so weightless that it
lifts water to it, does not sit
on the oily surface,
glosses surface,
like a balloon
whose belly
is lighter than the air
around it. Translated, it goes
in and through and out; in and through
and up in a cloth bubble that takes us
around the world in a fraction of eighty days;

the Himalayas, the hemispheres below us
   like a chain of glass beads; the Indies East and West
     in the seismic tremor of lifting a hand to the breeze; in the
     ease with which a world is glossed. The huge wave of
    an arm across a distant horizon; the gesture *here is*
where it all begins.

But the fortieth day finds our man Jesus
in the desert, his darkness settling him,
the light around him glowing,
refracting to show
the most
beautiful angel,
the great wings beating still,
the land spread before him.
The new world panorama. *Yours*
if you'll love me, the light
breathes.

We know the story: He eventually returns on a donkey
to the city that will kill him.
Martyrs always get it in the end,
but do grasshoppers?

I turn my head and say,
"Ah, grasshopper."
I turn my head
and say, "Ah,
grasshopper."

Hostage

Almond leaves the size of hands sweep the terrace
skirting the almonds felled by last night's storm.

A slick of water and crazy ants on a toppled fir sprig
decide to be an island and small sea.

Thunder still rumbles in the sound of trucks
pitching down the mountain's sides.

This morning I am held hostage by bougainvillea
which watch me ease into my skin.

Here I am betrayed only by the uncovered watch
band of my pale and diasporic self.

Time slows to make me primordial. *Kenèps*
make me five and confused as to why

the fruit does not yield its sweetness easily.
My mother's hand at my hand's age now draws

the fruit's flesh from its coarse covering. I am
handed a perfumed ball of sugar and destroyed

in a move a month later. Returned and now
a cousin once removed and former playmate

visits with her daughters. They are strangers
to me. Estelle, *la petite,* with adult teeth

explains, "Auntie's sad because she cannot chew
our words." I bite one to prove something to her.

The Yellow Forms of Paradise

With paradise suspended from their necks like a giant clock,
the old folks stitch together the island's shifting colors.

Its iridescent paths of light, they project onto the days between
this and the lost country. We are going back they say.

They pierce our ears with the golden studs of paradise which hum
when removed and studied in the palm. Home is a tiny bracelet

engraved with a girl's name, a scarf that ties the head down,
keeps it from flying. This yellow form of paradise, a disease,

an unlit road carved from fields sown with two sets of trees,
maple, palm, and we who we leap from one set to another

all the while seeking ground.

* * *

Vertigo is never fun the old folks say, you fall without falling,
at once at the building's edge and at its foot. Beyond the building

a mountain laughs and behind it another, snow-peaked and ready
to release its avalanche of beads. We roll them underfoot, throw

a goat knuckle up and catch it with another knuckle. We sweep
the streets with our hair and on clean sidewalks picket the use

of our blood abroad. We write the dead who return amid clouds.
To the living we rain our green love in letters post-marked by birds.

For the living we bow to the great creator of fragments and break
into pieces on airplanes. Three new skies suffocate my old clouds.

My soil grows anemic. It whispers to me: *Return.*

* * *

The ascent can be nitrogened with quick bubbles to the blood.
Do not rise too fast for surface, too fast for the beach road

for the path once river now stone. The gods ride this, color of blood,
color of earth, backwards from the hills. Uphill is a monument

of breaking coral. Uphill is a series of dead *caballeros*, uphill
is a salted plain whose dust reveals an army of cactus soldiers.

A topsoil of plastic bottles paves the way to the city of *peristyle*s,
to the city of seven million gods.

* * *

A *camionette* of color cries by. I count the carried. I count the hills.
I count the buried. The living sweep by with their tongues in baskets.

The living sweep by with their golden rings and *gwayabel*s. The living
sweep by with their canes and dusty shoes, their brooms and *mango fransik.*

The living squeak by greased in oil of palma christi, accompanied
by the *wiwa*s of donkeys. The returned sweep by with their double vision

and sunglasses of the dead. The returned sweep by with dirty hair.

* * *

Now, how can I give you up, my mother's earth, my alpha tongue?
I will bed this earth.   I will give birth to a three-headed child.

A mouth will emerge from my navel, another from my sex,
and a third from a third eye not mine.   Her lungs will be sound.

She will call me mother.

Notes

(page 19) *fout:* damn

(page 20) *majuscule:* capital (in reference to letters)

(page 21) *un et un/–deux/deux et deux/–quatre:* one and
one/–two/two and two/–four

(page 22) *an Kreyol:* in Creole

comment vas tuuu: how are youuu

eau: toilet water (Note: the author, with deep regret,
could not include the perennial Bien-Être among the
parfumes/eaux-de-toilet/santibons of "How to Kiss."
This due to reasons of line length. She begs the
forgiveness of all Bien-Être users.)

(page 23) *Un véritable scandale:* A veritable scandal

(page 27) *nos ancêtres, les Gaulois:* our ancestors, the Gauls
(phrase from a French children's history text, used
widely, until recently, in Francophone primary schools.

mystères: mysteries or gods (in Creole religious sense)

(page 30) *Haitiens:* Haitians

(page 36) *Anacaona:* The name of the poet and ruler of Xaragua,
one of the five regions of Ayiti (now Hispaniola) at the
time of Columbus's arrival in 1492. She sought to unite
the regions against the colonizers but was ambushed and
hanged in her attempt.

(page 37) *sanba:* poet, storyteller, or singer

(page 40) *Yvon Desanges* was a 27-year-old youth organizer and
vocal supporter of the democratic movement in Haiti,
murdered in the spring of 1994 in Port-au-Prince.

(page 43) *Fin Wè Mò:* Done Seen the Dead (literal translation, and
used in this sense in the poem. Typically translated as
relentless, enraged, or *infuriated*)

(page 44) *Les dents de la mer:* "Jaws" (French translation of the 1970s Peter Benchley novel, and film of the same name)

Pa Benyen Ni Ak Kilot Ni Ak Eslip: No Swimming in Underwear

Plaj Piblik: Public Beach

(page 54) *Compas:* French spelling of a Haitian musical genre

mouchoir: handkerchief

boutonnière: buttonhole (on lapel)

(page 55) *Fillette:* girl, lass

(page 66) *the great wings beating still:* A line from the W.B. Yeats poem "Leda and the Swan"

(page 67) *Kenèp:* honeyberry (a tropical fruit)

la petite: the little one

(page 69) *caballero:* horseman

peristyle: public section of a vodou sanctuary

gwayabel: A popular dress shirt, often short-sleeved

mango fransik: A variety of mango popular in Haiti

wiwa: Author's phonetic transcription of the sound a donkey makes

Special thanks:

Many thanks are due to the Georges and Legros families,
Sandy Taylor and Judy Doyle, Ernest Baroni, Tisa Bryant,
Grace Cambridge, Yolande Champagne, Charles Coe, Pourguichat Dave,
Muhonjia Khaminwa, Marilyn Levitt, Dahlma Llanos, Charlot Lucien,
Henri-Robert Martineau, Jean-Claude Martineau, Elizabeth McKim,
Smith Nazaire, Soo Jin Oh, Ketsia Théodore-Pharel, Della Scott,
Ilda St. Jean, Jennifer Trapp, Afaa Michael Weaver, and Zanset Yo.

***

I'm grateful to the following organizations for support, and the luxury
of time and space: The MacDowell Artists Colony, the Barbara Deming
Memorial Fund, the Harmony Women's Fund, The Caribbean Writers
Summer Institute (University of Miami), and the Writers' Room of
Boston.

***

Thank you to: The Dark Room Collective; the Harvard Law School
Publications Center Staff; The Joiner Center (University of
Massachusetts, Boston); *compost*; Lorna Goodison; the New York
University Creative Writing Department; the spirit of BlaWoWow;
Angie Cruz and the women of WILL; Edwidge Danticat, PEN New
England; Women Writers of Haitian Descent; and M23, Brooklyn.

CURBSTONE PRESS, INC.

is a non-profit publishing house dedicated to literature that reflects a commitment to social change, with an emphasis on contemporary writing from Latino, Latin American and Vietnamese cultures. Curbstone presents writers who give voice to the unheard in a language that goes beyond denunciation to celebrate, honor and teach. Curbstone builds bridges between its writers and the public – from inner-city to rural areas, colleges to community centers, children to adults. Curbstone seeks out the highest aesthetic expression of the dedication to human rights and intercultural understanding: poetry, testimonies, novels, stories, and children's books.

This mission requires more than just producing books. It requires ensuring that as many people as possible learn about these books and read them. To achieve this, a large portion of Curbstone's schedule is dedicated to arranging tours and programs for its authors, working with public school and university teachers to enrich curricula, reaching out to underserved audiences by donating books and conducting readings and community programs, and promoting discussion in the media. It is only through these combined efforts that literature can truly make a difference.

Curbstone Press, like all non-profit presses, depends on the support of individuals, foundations, and government agencies to bring you, the reader, works of literary merit and social significance which might not find a place in profit-driven publishing channels, and to bring the authors and their books into communities across the country. Our sincere thanks to the many individuals, foundations, and government agencies who support this endeavor: J. Walton Bissell Foundation, Connecticut Commission on the Arts, Connecticut Humanities Council, Daphne Seybolt Culpeper Foundation, Fisher Foundation, Greater Hartford Arts Council, Hartford Courant Foundation, J. M. Kaplan Fund, Eric Mathieu King Fund, John D. and Catherine T. MacArthur Foundation, National Endowment for the Arts, Open Society Institute, Puffin Foundation, and the Woodrow Wilson National Fellowship Foundation.

Please help to support Curbstone's efforts to present the diverse voices and views that make our culture richer. Tax-deductible donations can be made by check or credit card to:
Curbstone Press, 321 Jackson Street, Willimantic, CT 06226
phone: (860) 423-5110   fax: (860) 423-9242
www.curbstone.org

IF YOU WOULD LIKE TO BE A MAJOR SPONSOR OF A
CURBSTONE BOOK, PLEASE CONTACT US.